AL•LEONARD®

PIANO PLAY-ALONG

AUDIO
ACCESS
INCLUDED

PLAYBACK+
Speed • Pitch • Balance • Loop

PIANO | VOCAL | GUITAR • AUDIO   VOLUME 65

CASTING CROWNS

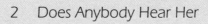

T0081971

Cover photo: Jeremy Cowart

To access audio visit:
www.halleonard.com/mylibrary

Enter Code
1211-2907-7208-0042

ISBN 978-1-4234-3481-8

HAL•LEONARD®
CORPORATION
7777 W. BLUEMOUND RD. P.O. BOX 13819 MILWAUKEE, WI 53213

Visit Hal Leonard Online at
www.halleonard.com

DOES ANYBODY HEAR HER

Words and Music by
MARK HALL

Moderately

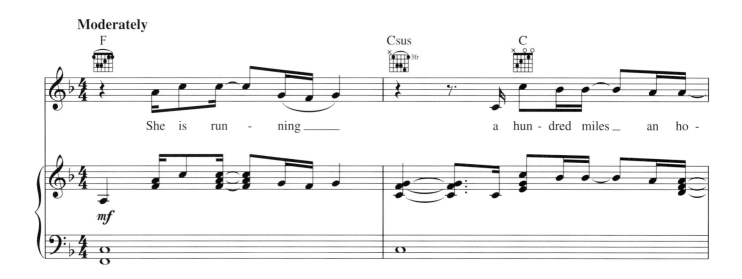

She is run - ning _____ a hun - dred miles _ an ho-

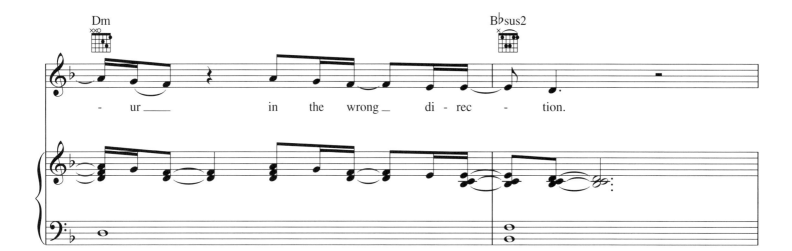

- ur _____ in the wrong _ di - rec - tion.

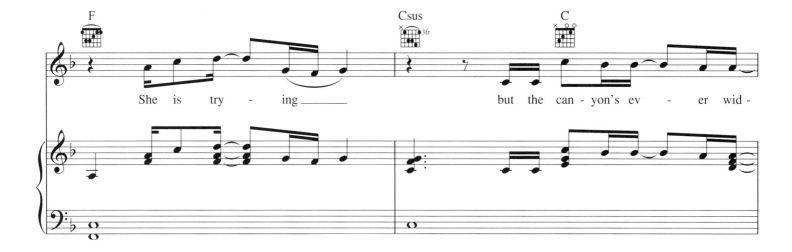

She is try - ing _____ but the can - yon's ev - er wid-

'ning in the depths of her cold heart. So she
sets out on an-oth-er mis-ad-ven-ture, just to find she's an-
oth-er two years old-er and she's three more steps be-hind.

Does an-y-bod-y hear her? Can an-y-bod-y see?

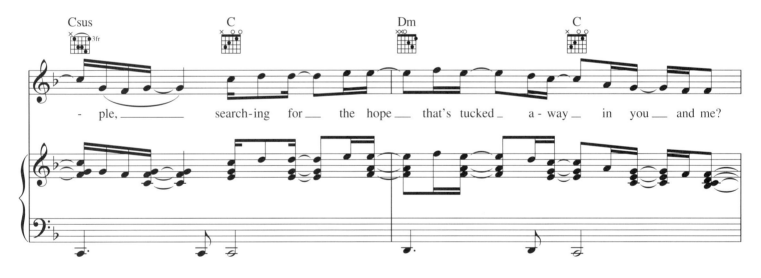

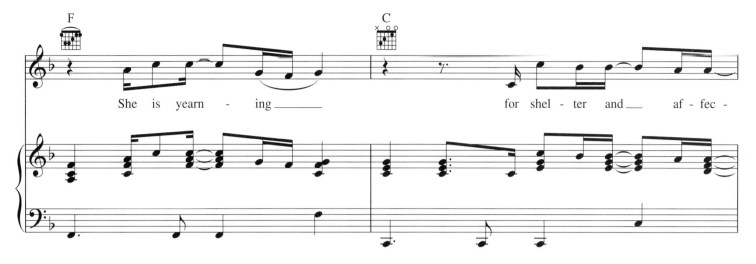

She is yearn - ing _____ for shel - ter and __ af - fec -

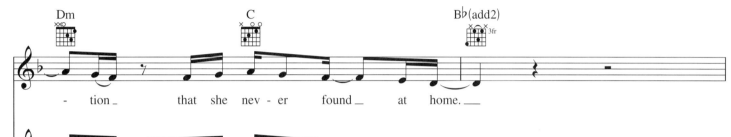

- tion __ that she nev - er found __ at home. __

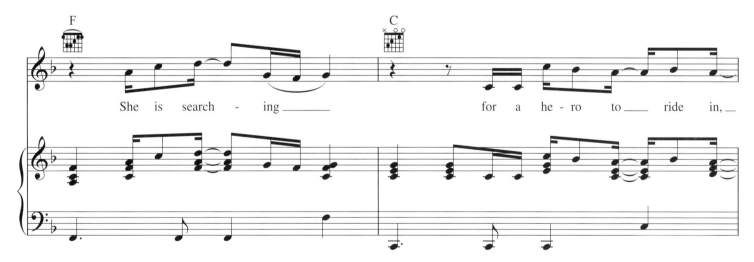

She is search - ing _____ for a he - ro to __ ride in, __

__ to ride in and save __ the day. __

And

you can't see past her scar - let let - ter, and we nev - er e – ven met __ her.

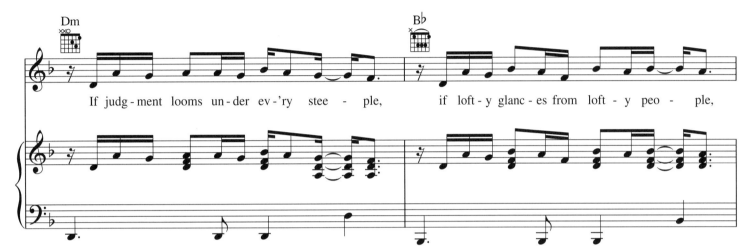

If judg - ment looms un - der ev -'ry stee - ple, if loft - y glanc - es from loft - y peo - ple,

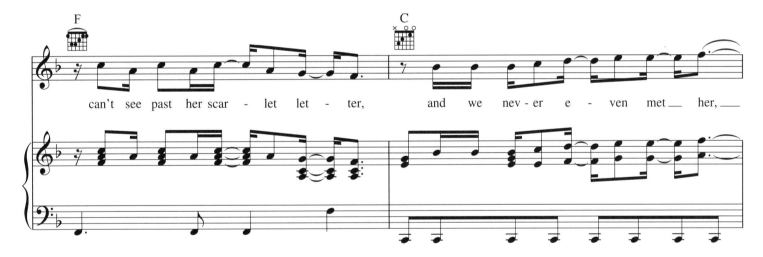

can't see past her scar - let let - ter, and we nev - er e – ven met __ her, __

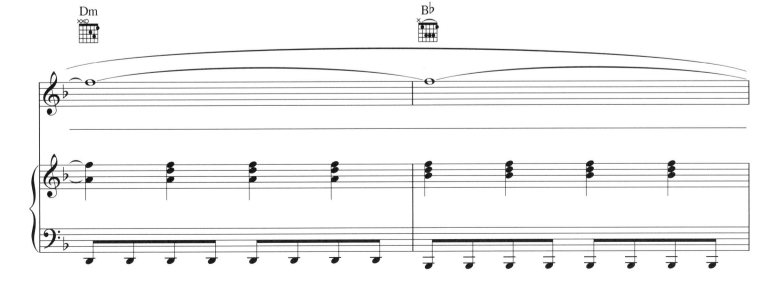

nev-er e - ven met her._____ Does an - y-bod - y hear____

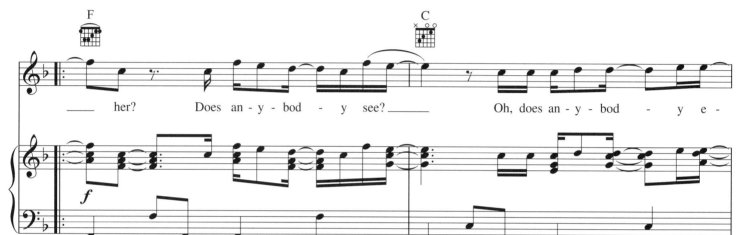

____ her? Does an-y-bod - y see?_____ Oh, does an-y-bod - y e-

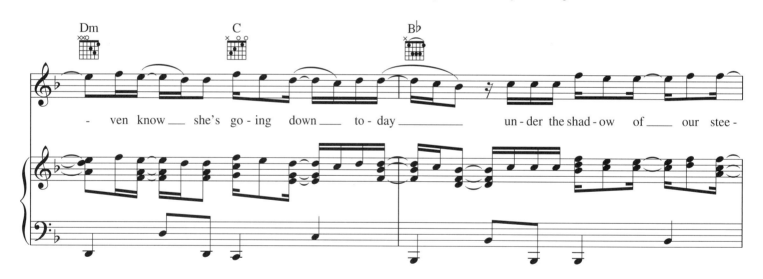

- ven know ___ she's go-ing down ___ to-day _____ un-der the shad-ow of ___ our stee-

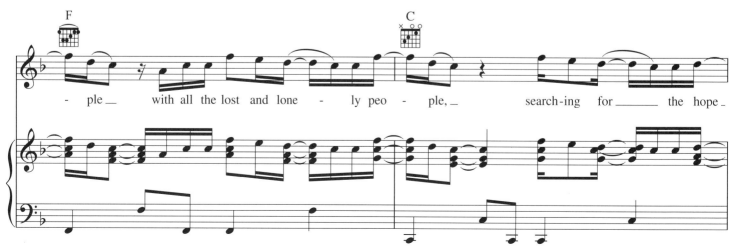

- ple ___ with all the lost and lone - ly peo - ple, ___ search-ing for _____ the hope ___

EAST TO WEST

Words and Music by MARK HALL
and BERNIE HERMS

Moderate Rock beat

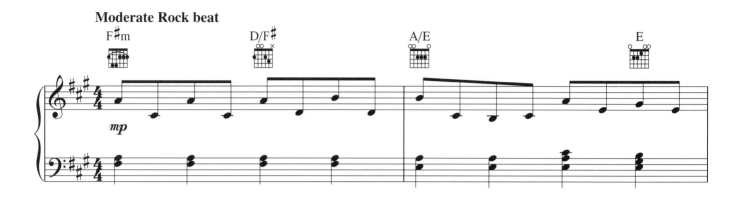

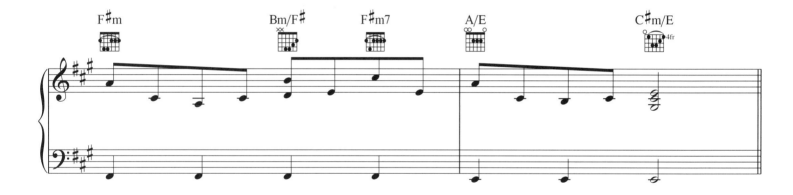

Here I am, __ Lord, and __ I'm drown - ing in Your sea of for - get - ful - ness. __

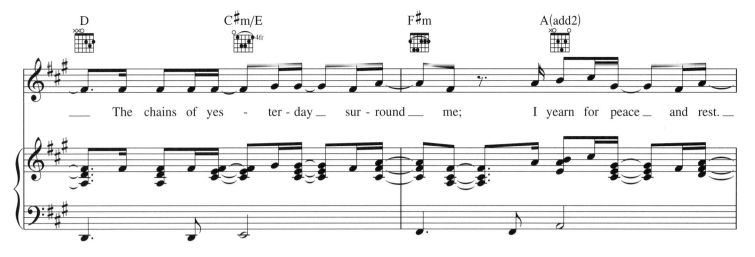

The chains of yes - ter - day__ sur - round__ me; I yearn for peace__ and rest.__

I don't want to end up where__ You found__ me, and it ech - oes in__ my mind,__

keeps me a - wake__ to - night.__

I know You've cast__ my sin__ as far__ as the east__ is from the west,__

and I stand be-fore you now ___ as, as though I've nev-er sinned.

But to-day I feel ___ like I'm just one mis-take ___ a - way ___ from You

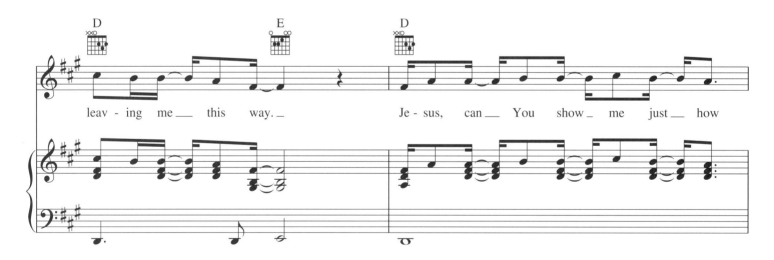

leav - ing me ___ this way. ___ Je - sus, can ___ You show ___ me just ___ how

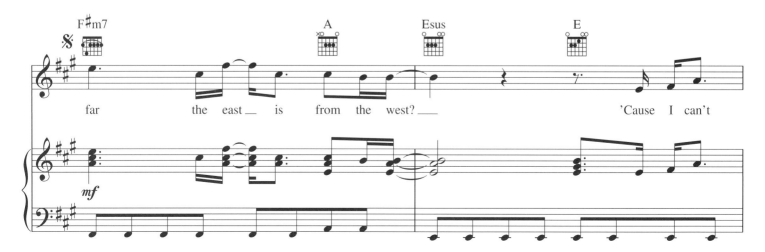

far the east ___ is from the west? ___ 'Cause I can't

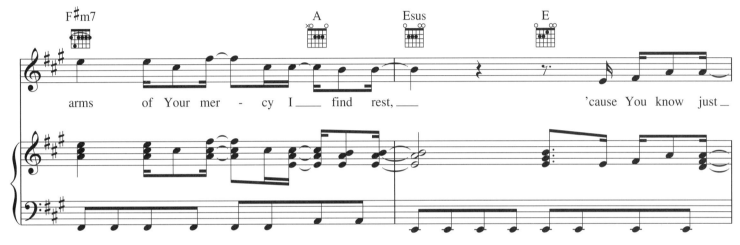

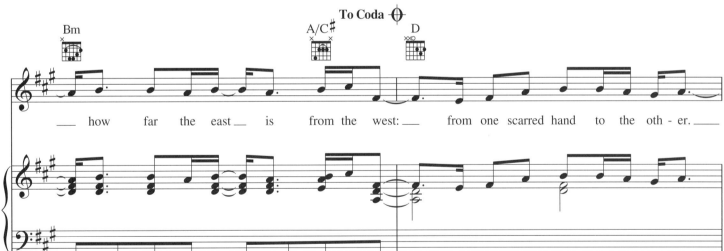

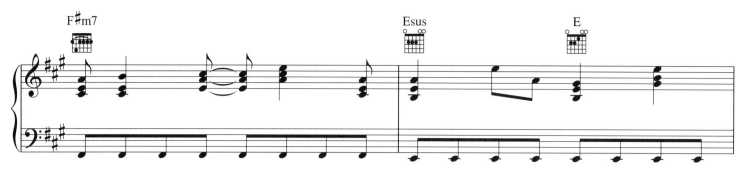

I start the day,__ the war__ be - gins,__ end - less re - mind - ing of __ my sin. __

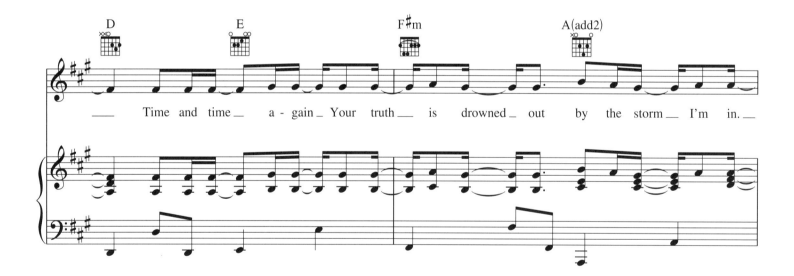

__ Time and time__ a - gain__ Your truth __ is drowned__ out by the storm__ I'm in. __

__ To - day I feel__ like I'm just __ one mis - take__ a - way__ from You

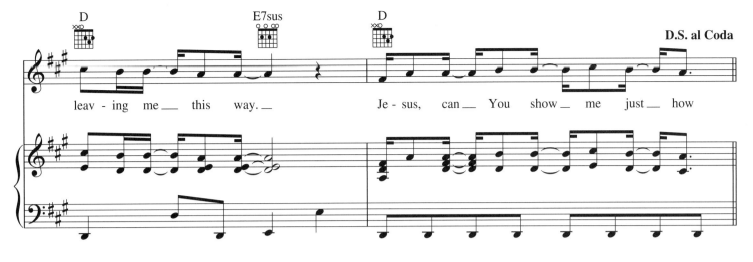

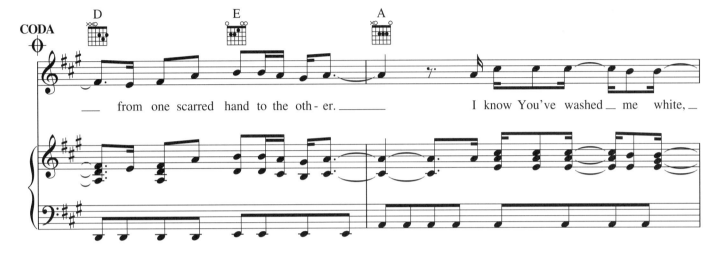

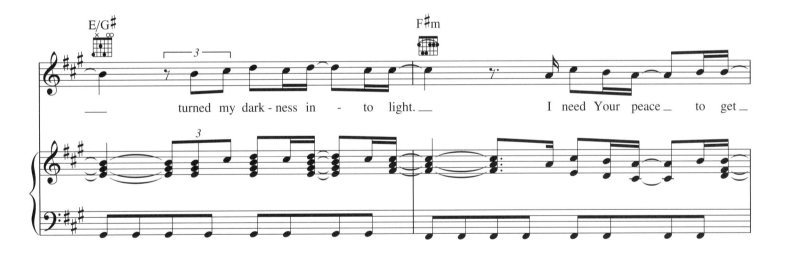

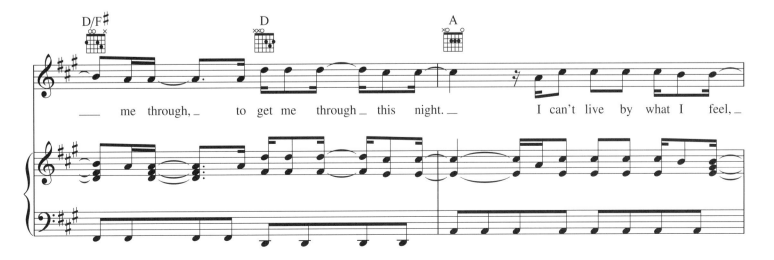

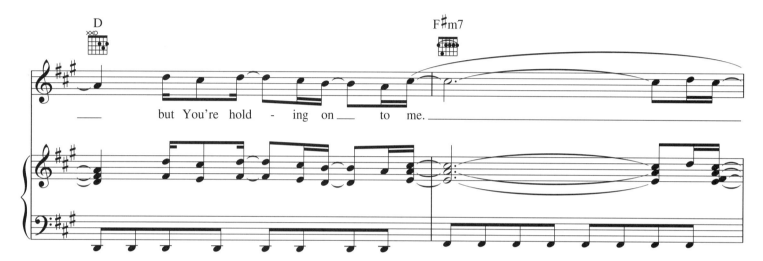

but by the truth Your Word __ re - veals. __ I'm not hold - ing on __ to You, __

but You're hold - ing on __ to me. __

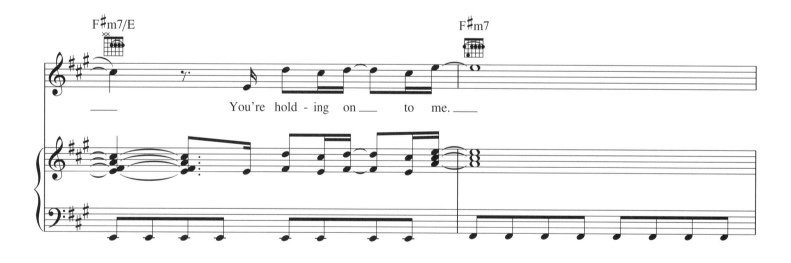

You're hold - ing on __ to me. __

Je - sus, You __ know just __ how far the east __ is from the west. __

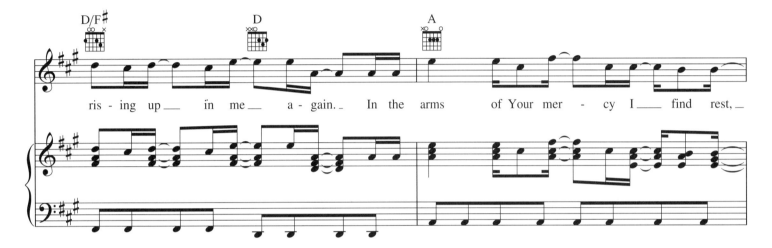

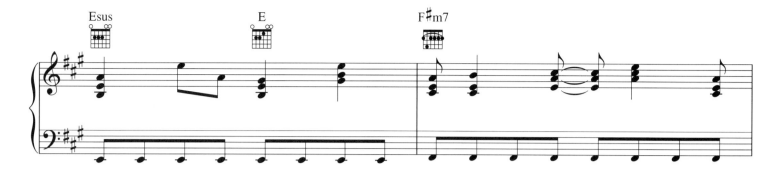

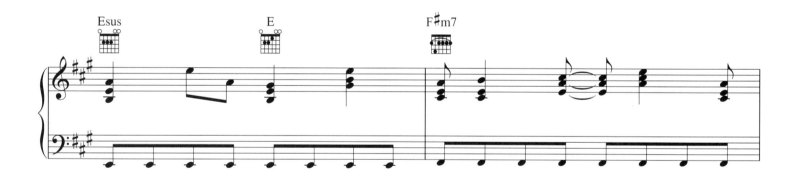

One scarred hand to the oth - er. _____

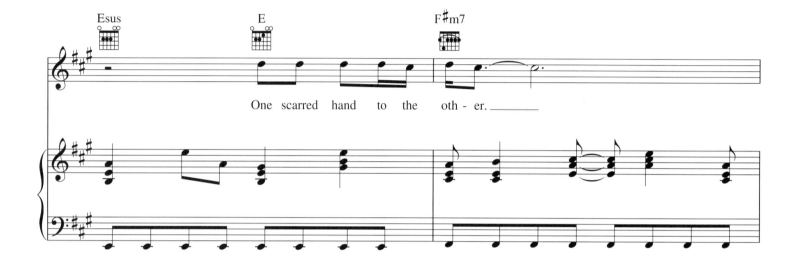

From one scarred hand to the oth - er. _____

PRAISE YOU IN THIS STORM

Words and Music by MARK HALL
and BERNIE HERMS

*Recorded a half step higher.

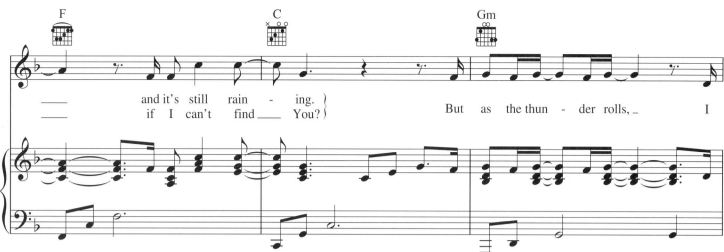

and it's still rain - ing.
if I can't find ___ You?
But as the thun - der rolls, ___ I

bare - ly hear ___ You whis-per through ___ the rain, ___ "I'm with ___ you." ___ And

as Your mer - cy falls, ___ I raise my hands ___ and praise the God ___ who gives ___

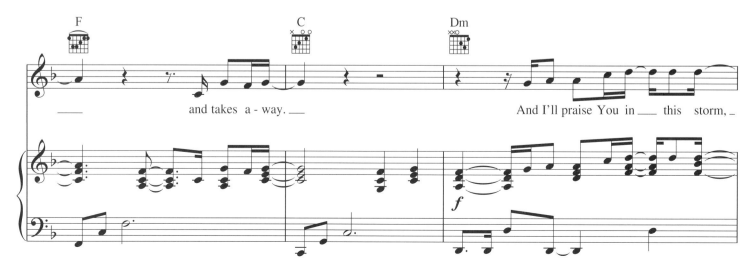

___ and takes a - way. ___ And I'll praise You in ___ this storm, ___ I

and I will lift ___ my hands, ___ for You are who ___ You are, ___

no mat - ter where ___ I am. ___ And ev - 'ry tear ___ I've cried ___

You hold in ___ Your hand. ___ You nev - er left ___ my side. ___

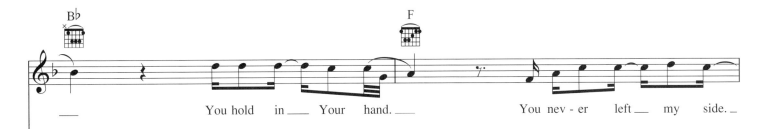

And though my heart ___ is torn, ___ I will praise You in ___ this storm. ___

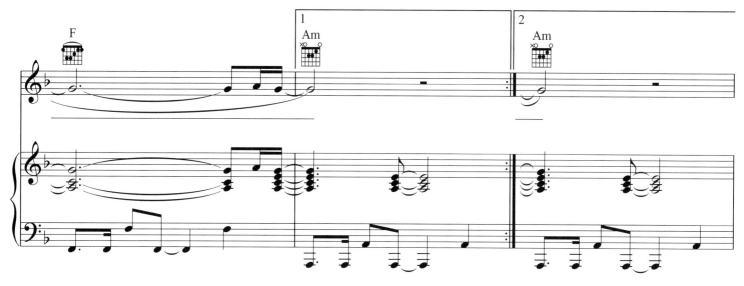

I praise You in ___ this storm.

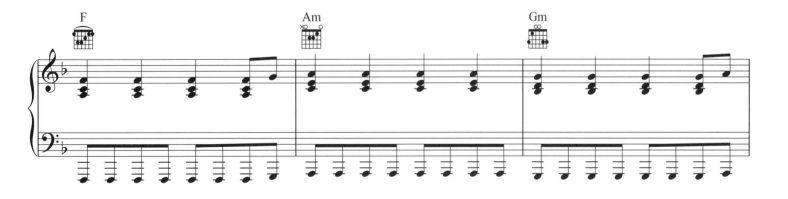

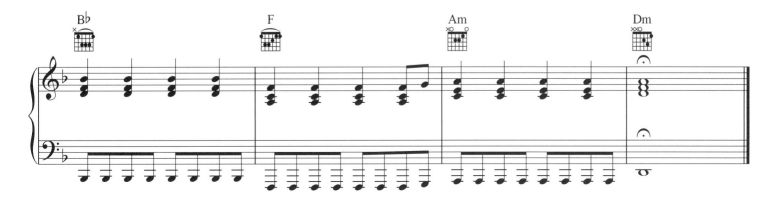

HERE I GO AGAIN

Words and Music by
MARK HALL

Moderately slow, in 1

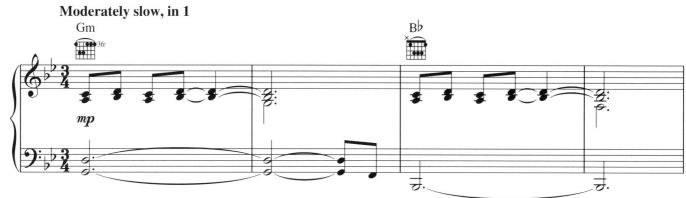

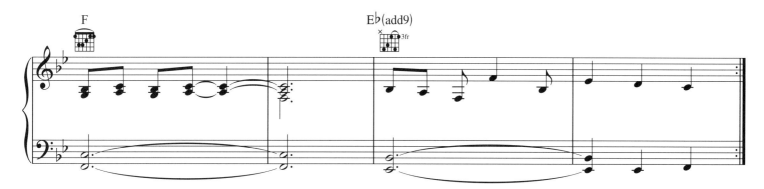

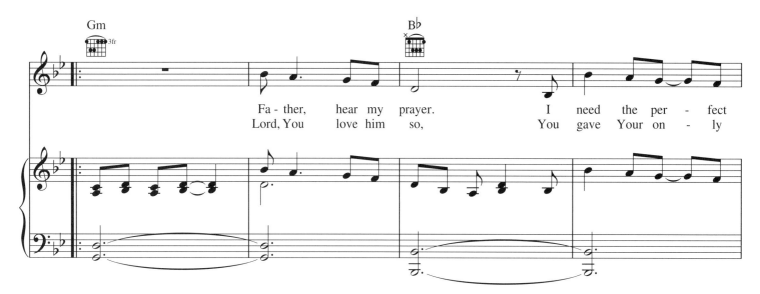

Fa - ther, hear my prayer. I need the per - fect
Lord, You love him so, You gave Your on - ly

words, I words that he will hear and
Son. If he will just be - lieve,

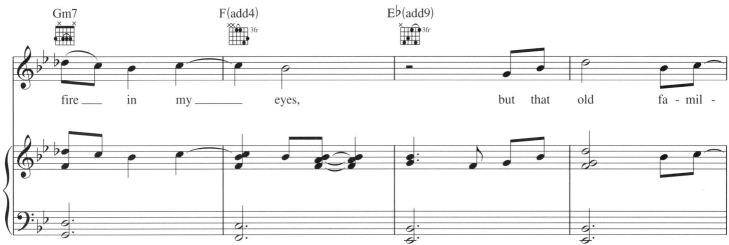

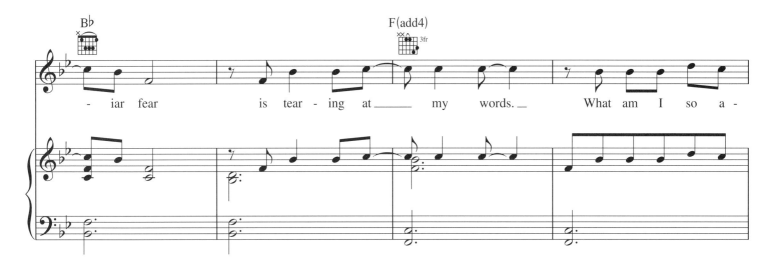

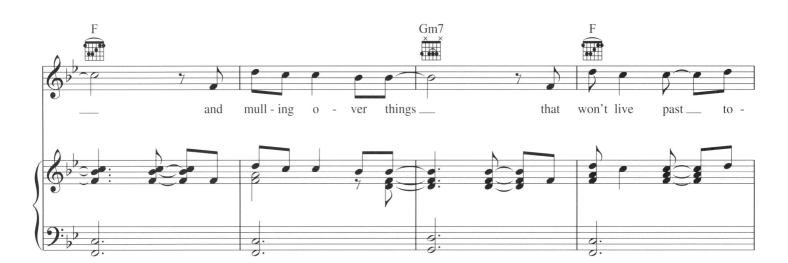

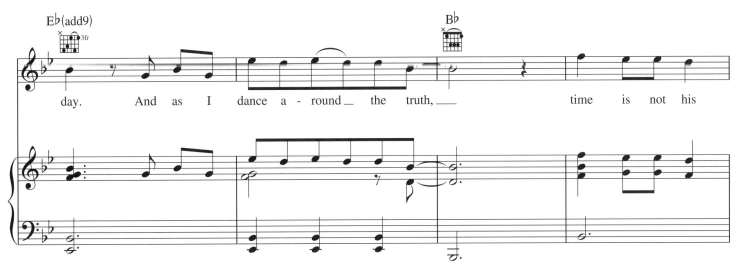

day. And as I dance a-round __ the truth, __ time is not his

friend. This might be ___ my last ___ chance to tell him that You love __

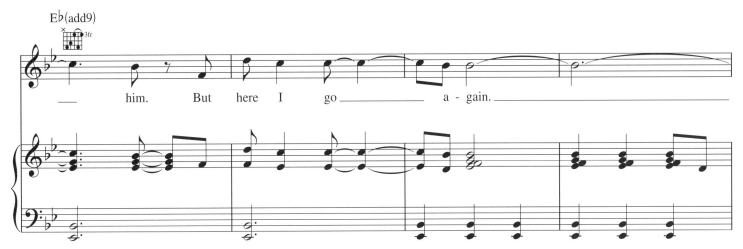

___ him. But here I go _____ a-gain. _____

Here I go _____ a-gain.

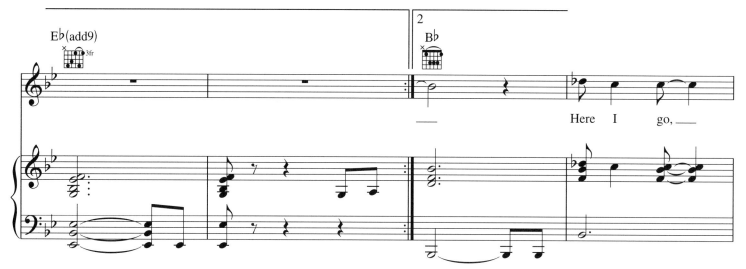

Eb(add9)   Bb

Here I go, __

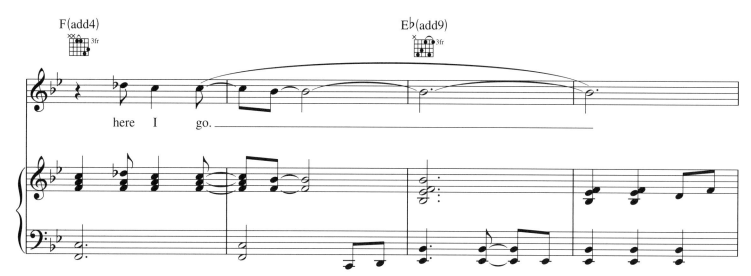

F(add4)   Eb(add9)

here I go. _____

Gm   Bb

F   Eb(add9)

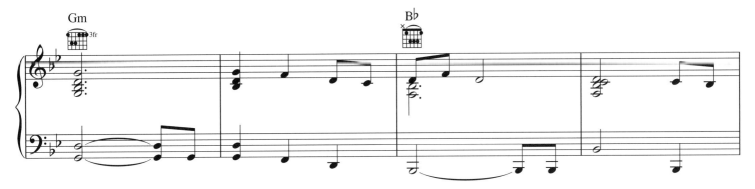

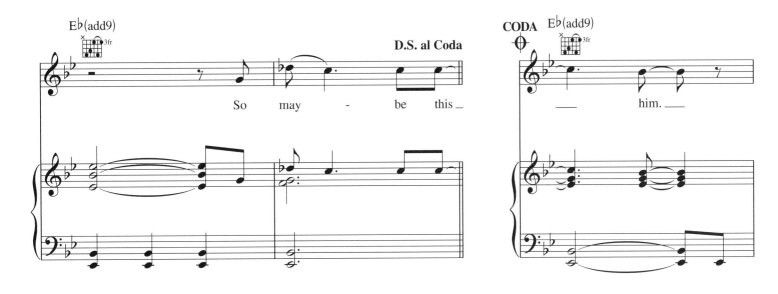

So may - be this ___

him. ___

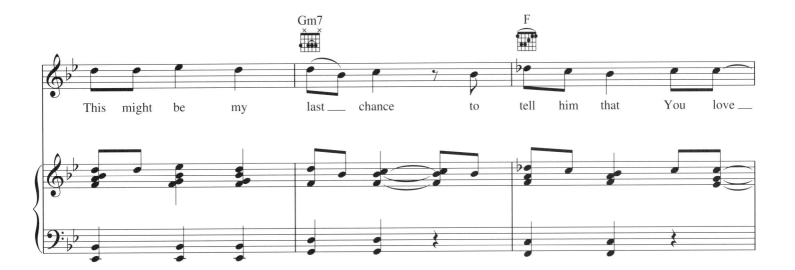

This might be my last ___ chance to tell him that You love ___

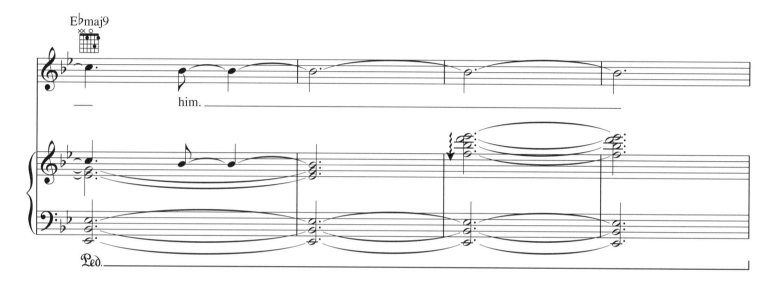

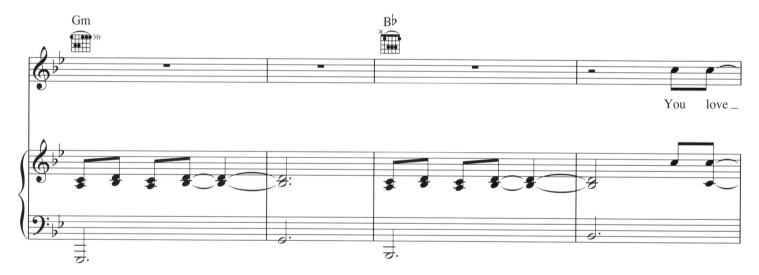

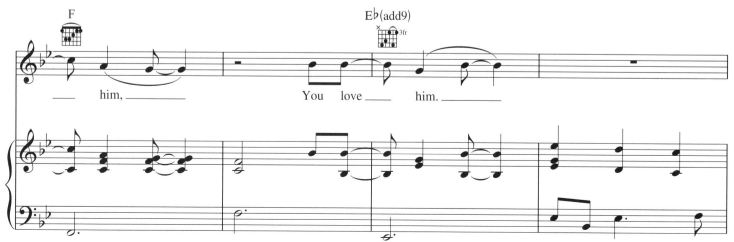

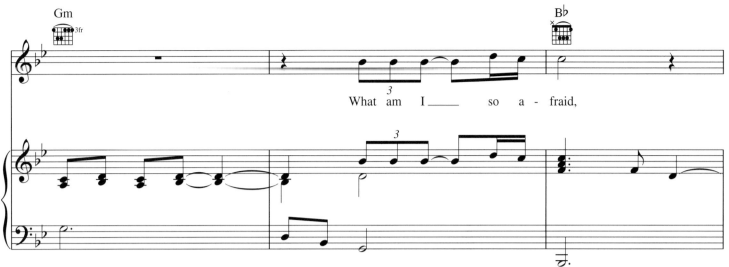

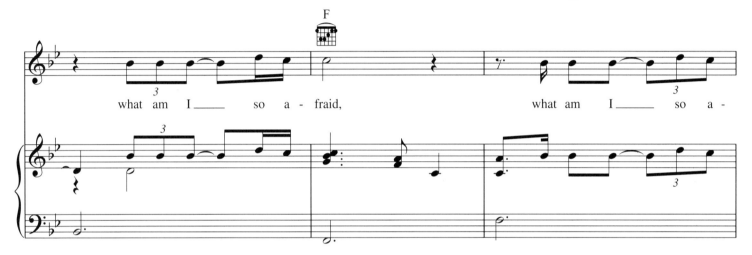

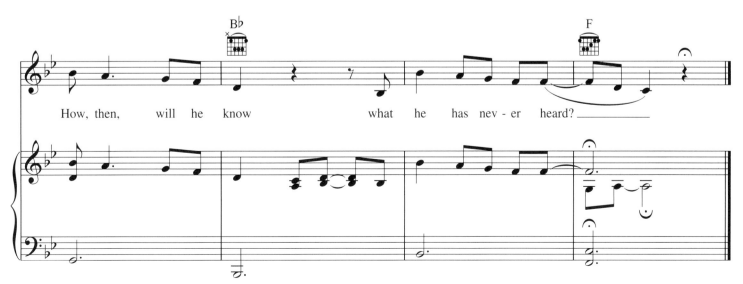

SOMEWHERE IN THE MIDDLE

Words and Music by
MARK HALL

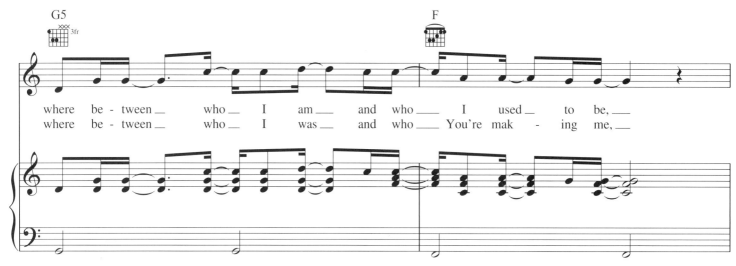

*Recorded a half step lower.

some - where in ___ the mid - dle you'll find ___ me. Some -
some - where in ___ the mid - dle you'll find ___

___ me. Just how close can I get, ___ Lord, to my sur - ren - der

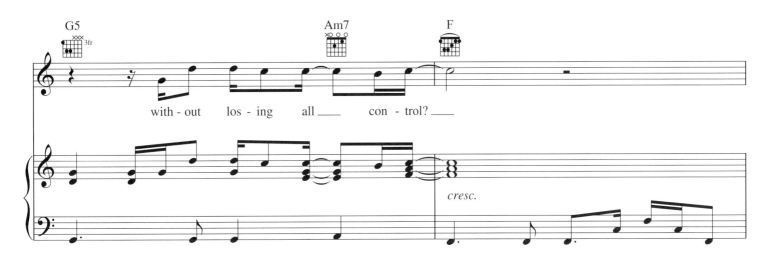

with - out los - ing all ___ con - trol? ___

Fear - less war - riors in a pick - et fence, ___ reck - less a - ban - don wrapped in ___ com - mon sense, ___

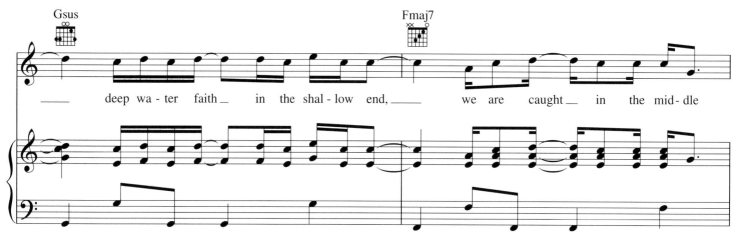

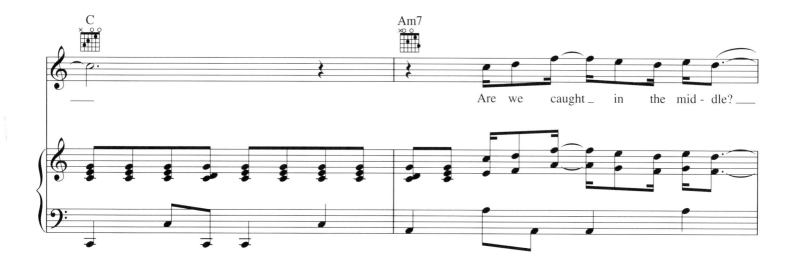

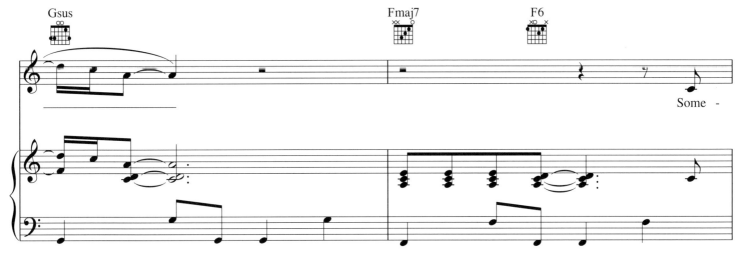

where be - tween __ a whis - per and __ a roar, _____ some -

where be - tween __ the al - tar and __ the door, _____ some -

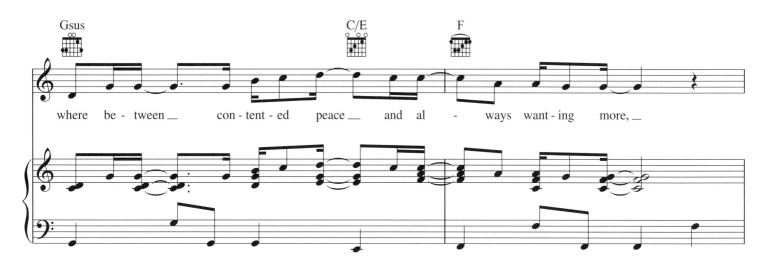

where be - tween __ con - tent - ed peace __ and al - ways want - ing more, __

some - where in ___ the mid - dle You'll find _____ me.

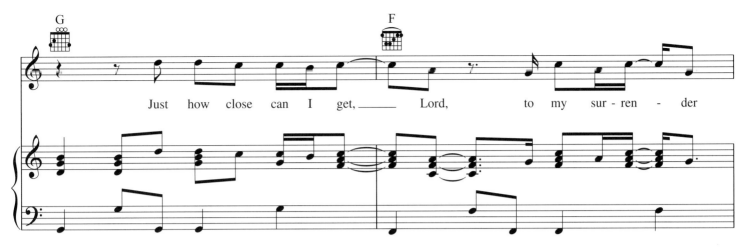

Just how close can I get, _____ Lord, to my sur - ren - der

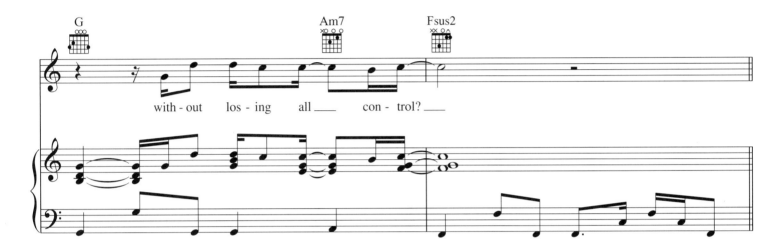

with - out los - ing all ___ con - trol? ___

Fear - less war - riors in a pick - et fence, __ reck - less a - ban - don wrapped in ___ com - mon sense, ___

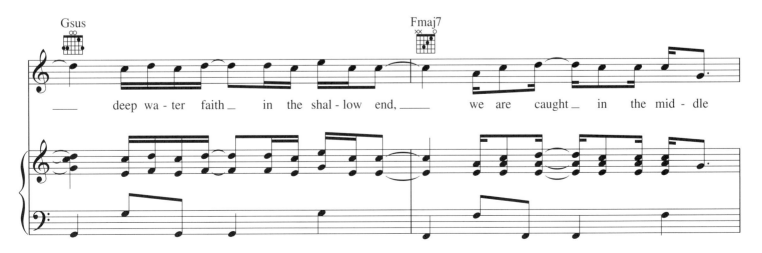

___ deep wa - ter faith _ in the shal - low end, _____ we are caught _ in the mid - dle

With eyes wide o - pen to the dif - f'renc - es, ___ the God we want ___ and the God ___ who is. ___

___ But will we trade ___ our dreams ___ for His, ___ or are we caught ___ in the mid - dle?

___ or are we caught ___ in the mid - dle? Lord, I feel ___ You in ___ this place, ___

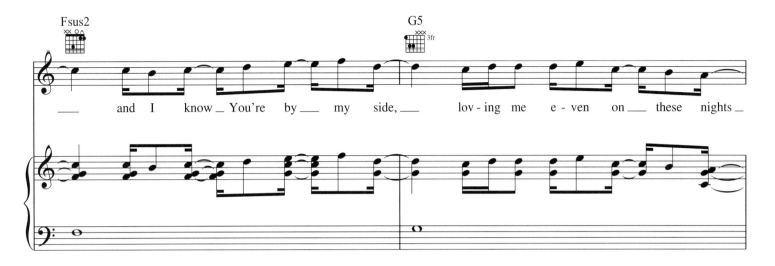

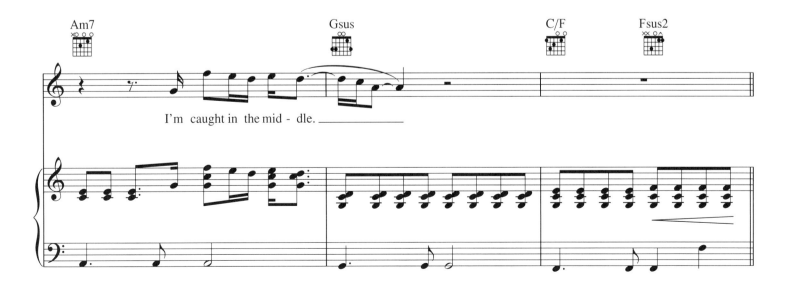

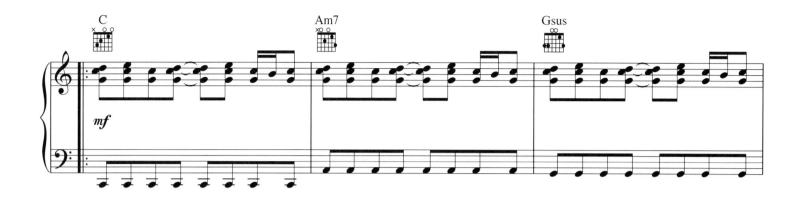

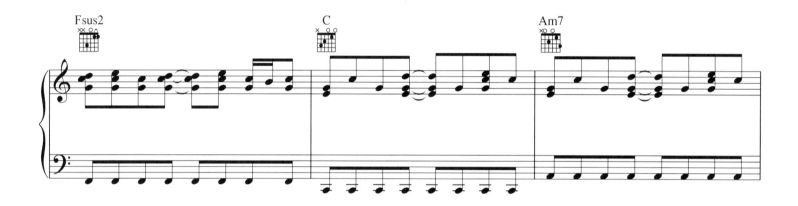

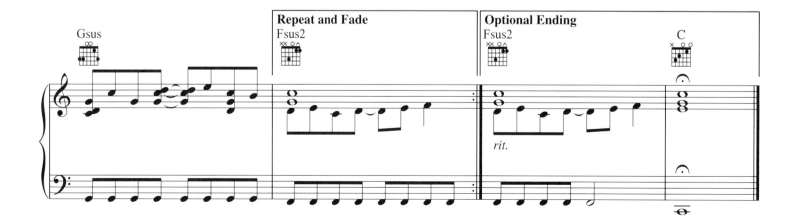

WHILE YOU WERE SLEEPING

Words and Music by
MARK HALL

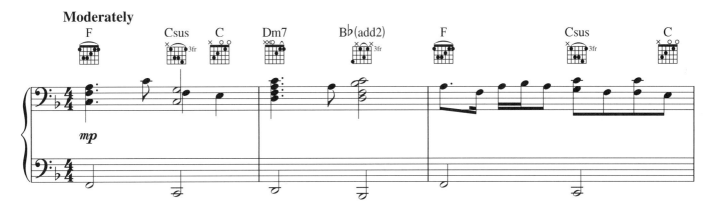

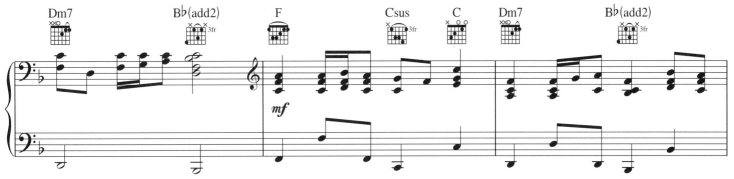

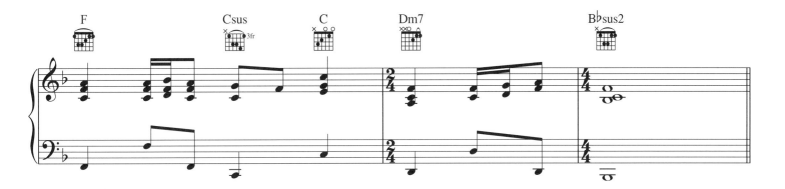

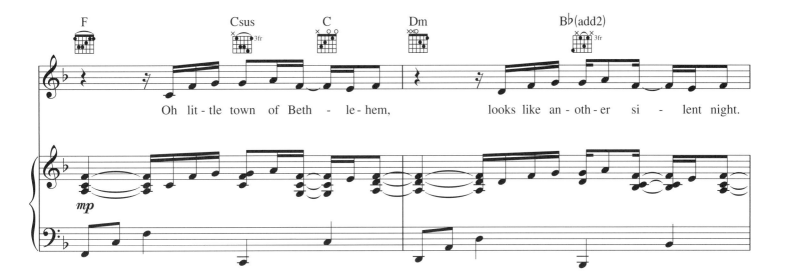

Oh lit-tle town of Beth - le-hem, looks like an-oth-er si - lent night.

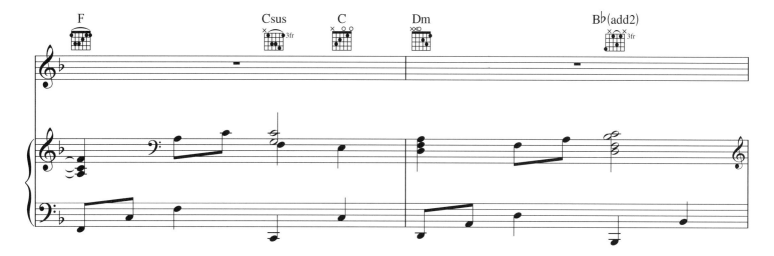

A - bove your deep __ and dream - less sleep, __ a gi - ant star __ lights up the sky. __

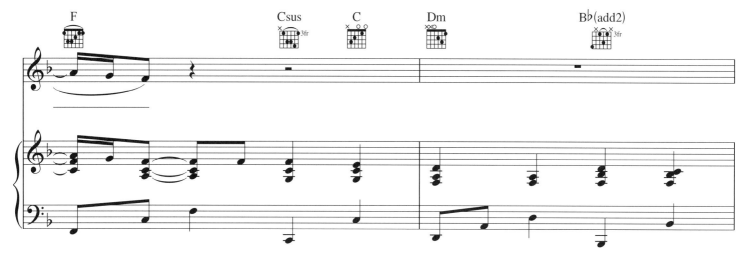

And while you're ly - ing in __ the dark, __ there shines an ev - er - last-

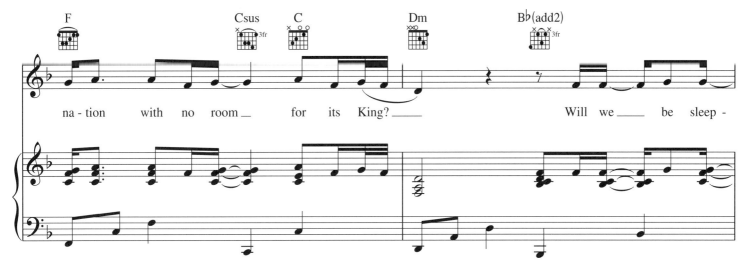

na - tion with no room __ for its King? ___ Will we __ be sleep -

- ing? __ Will we __ be sleep - ing? _____

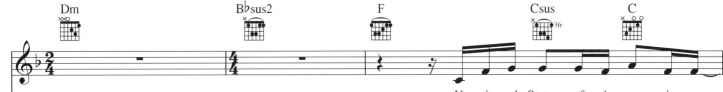

U - nit - ed States of A - mer - i - ca, __

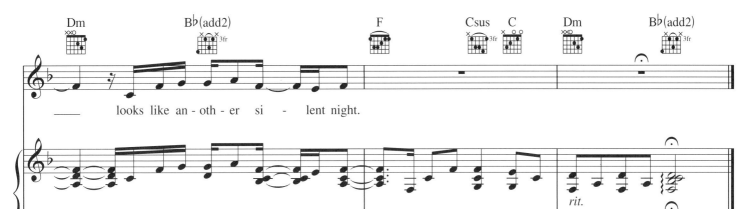

___ looks like an - oth - er si - lent night.

VOICE OF TRUTH

Words and Music by MARK HALL
and STEVEN CURTIS CHAPMAN

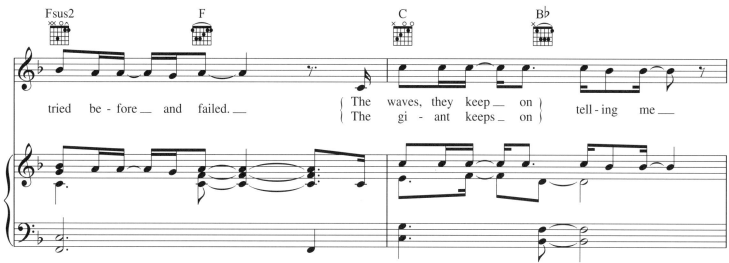

tried be-fore ___ and failed. ___ { The waves, they keep ___ on } tell-ing me ___
{ The gi-ant keeps ___ on }

time and time ___ a-gain, ___ "Boy, ___ you'll nev-er win!" "You'll

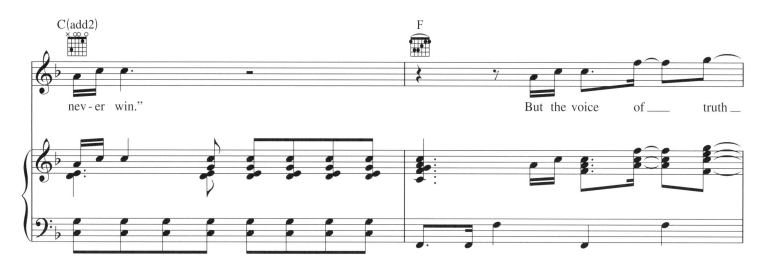

nev-er win." But the voice of ___ truth ___

___ tells me a dif-f'rent sto - ry. The voice of ___ truth ___

says, "Do not be ___ a - fraid." ___ And the voice of ___ truth ___

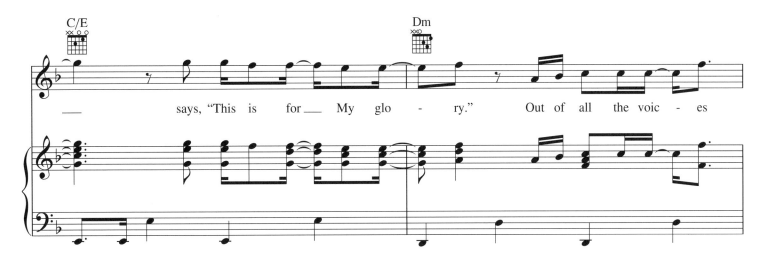

___ says, "This is for ___ My glo - ry." Out of all the voic - es

call - ing out ___ to ___ me, ___ I will choose ___ to lis -

To Coda

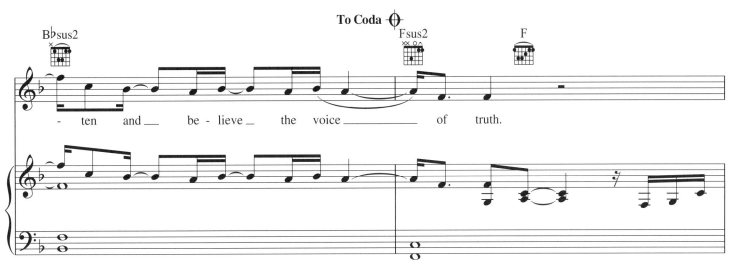

- ten and ___ be - lieve ___ the voice ___ of truth.

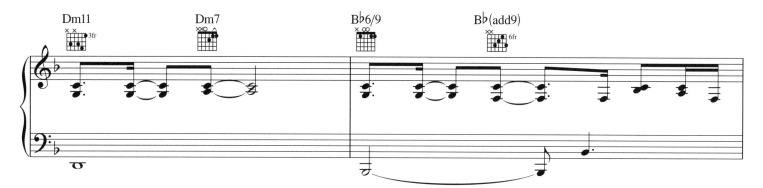

Oh, what I ____ would do ____ to have the

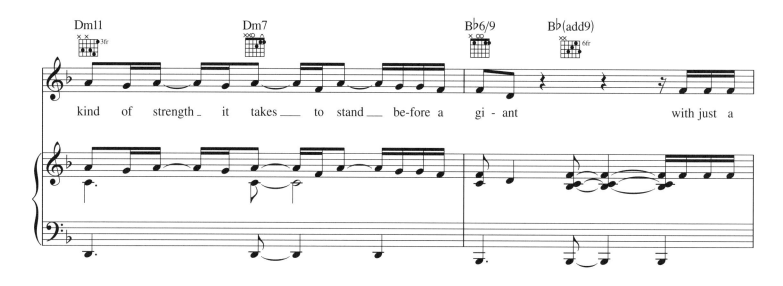

kind of strength __ it takes ____ to stand __ be-fore a gi - ant with just a

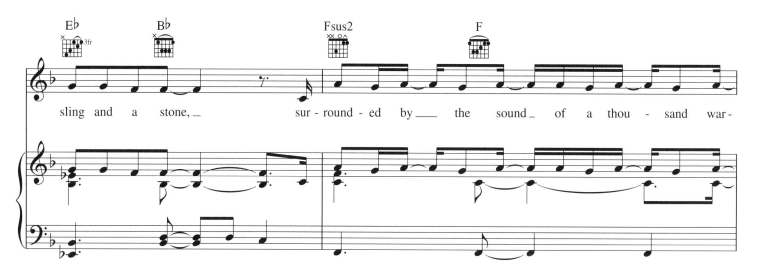

sling and a stone, __ sur - round - ed by ___ the sound __ of a thou - sand war-

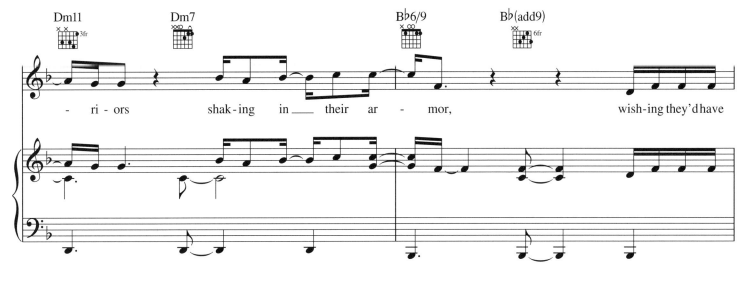

-ri-ors shak-ing in ___ their ar - mor, wish-ing they'd have

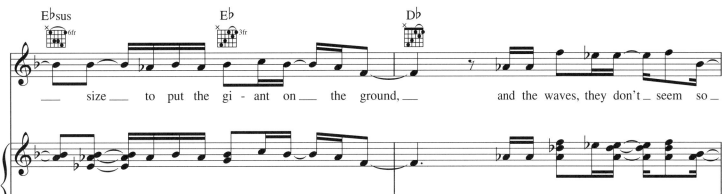

had the strength ___ to stand. ___ But the ___ of truth. But the stone was just the right ___

D.S. al Coda

CODA

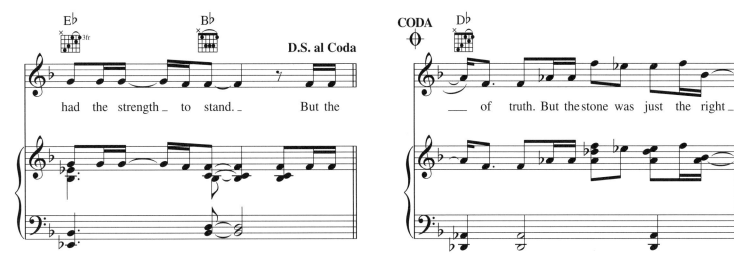

___ size ___ to put the gi - ant on ___ the ground, ___ and the waves, they don't ___ seem so ___

___ high from on top of them look-ing down. ___ I will soar with the wings of ea -

- gles when I stop __ and lis-ten to ___ the sound __ of Je - sus

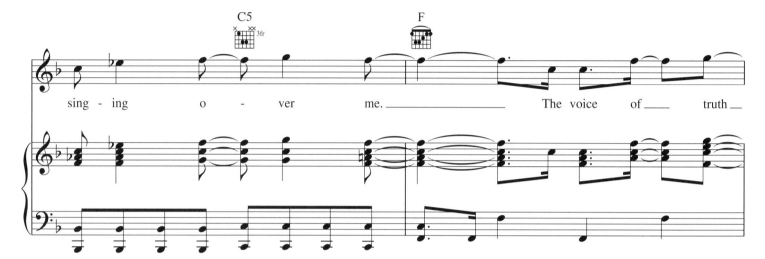

sing - ing o - ver me. _____ The voice of ___ truth ___

___ tells me a dif-f'rent sto - ry. The voice of ___ truth ___

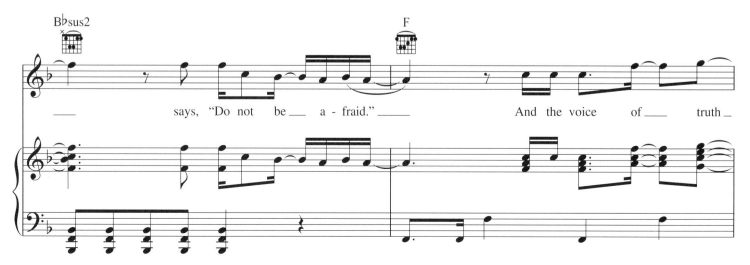

___ says, "Do not be __ a - fraid." _____ And the voice of ___ truth ___

says, "This is for __ My glo - ry." Out of all the voic - es

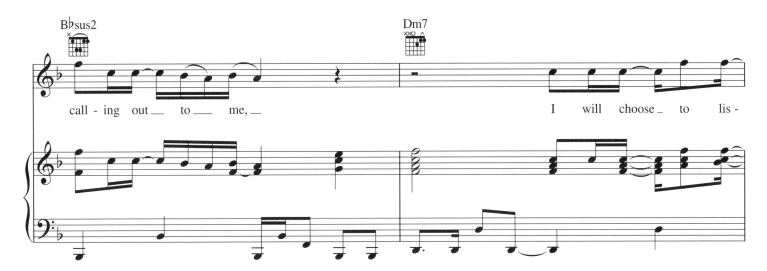

call - ing out __ to __ me, __ I will choose __ to lis -

- ten and __ be - lieve, _____ I will choose __ to lis -

- ten and __ be - lieve __ the voice _____

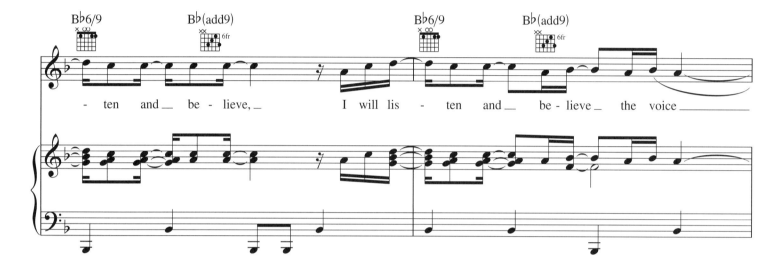

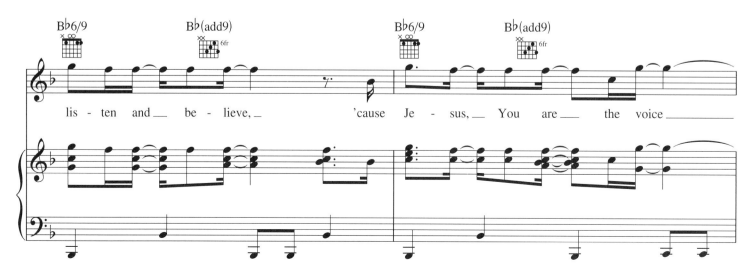

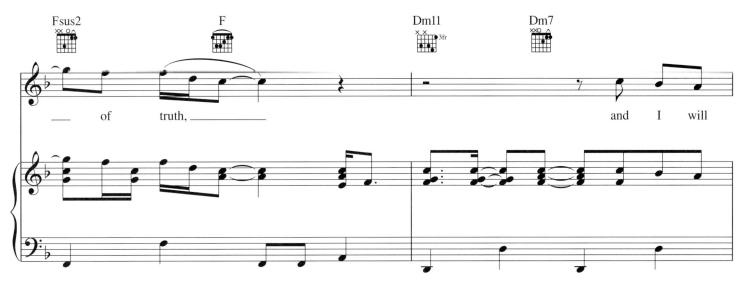

of truth, _____ and I will

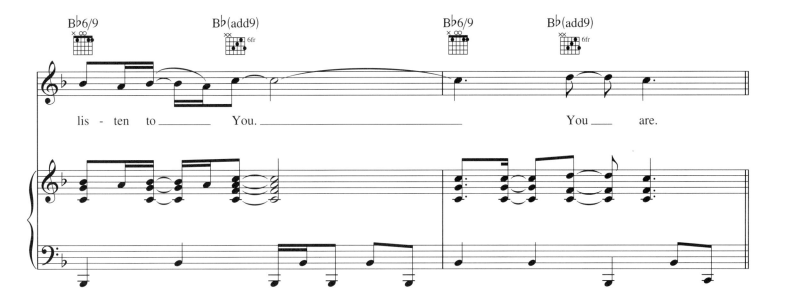

lis - ten to _____ You. _____ You ___ are.

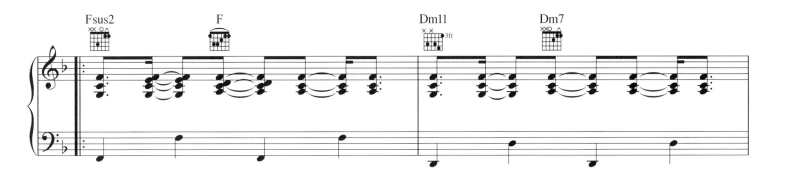

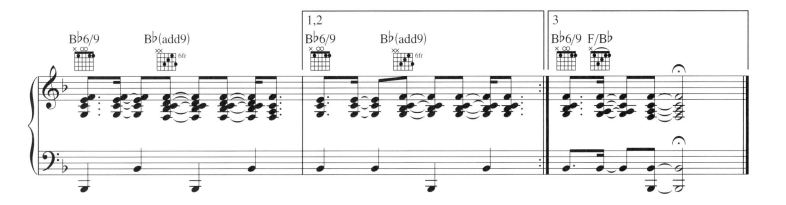

WHO AM I

Words and Music by
MARK HALL

Moderately slow, in 2

Who am I

— that the Lord of all the earth would
— that the eyes that see my sin would

care to know my name, would care to feel my hurt?
look on me with love and watch me rise a - gain?

* Recorded a half step higher.

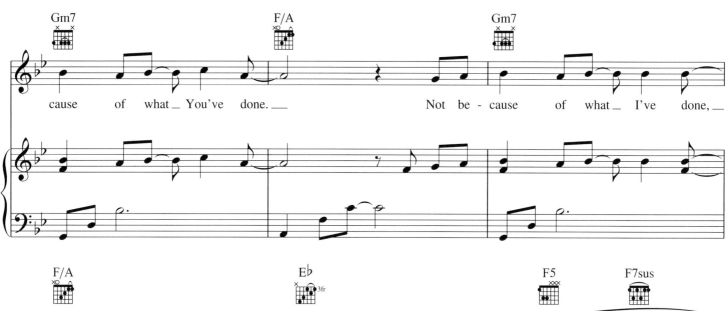

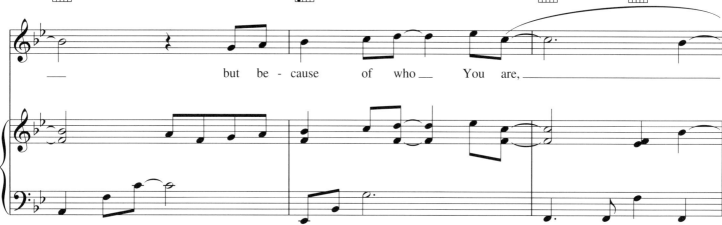

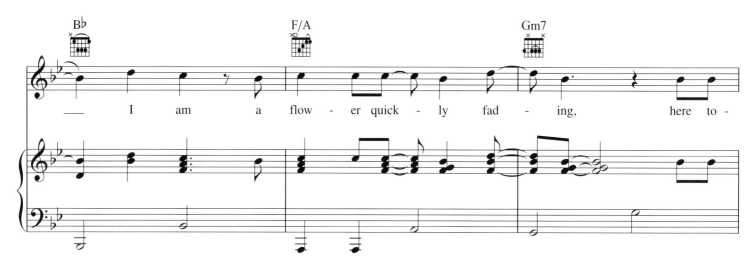

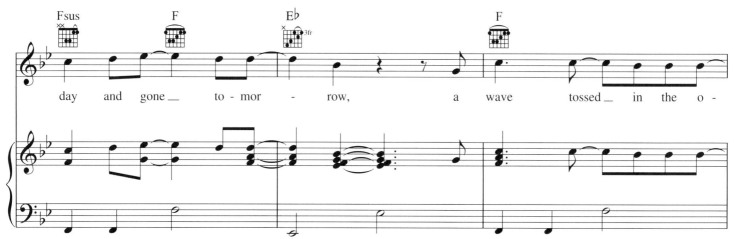

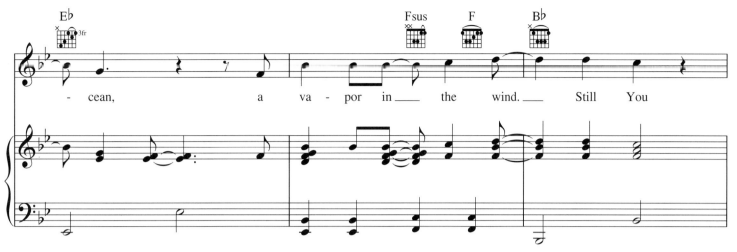

-cean, a va-por in __ the wind. __ Still You

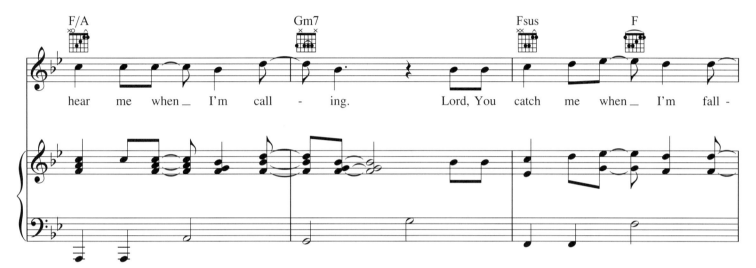

hear me when __ I'm call - ing. Lord, You catch me when __ I'm fall -

-ing and You've told me who __ I am: ___

I am Yours. ___ I am Yours. __

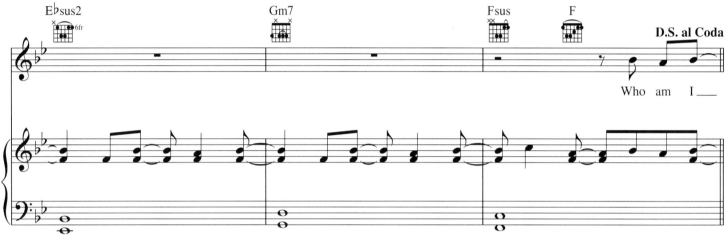

Who am I ___

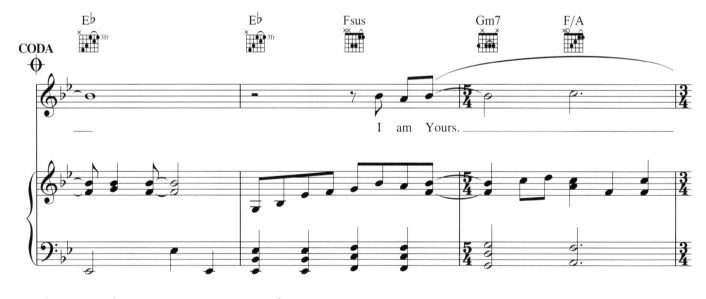

I am Yours. ___

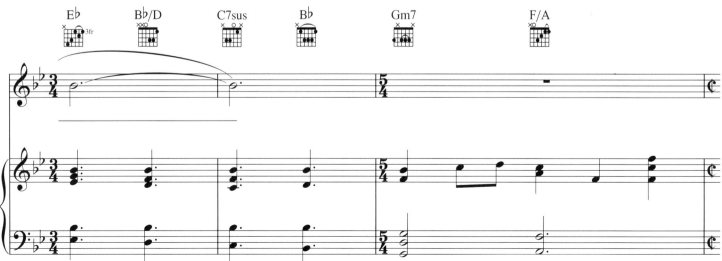

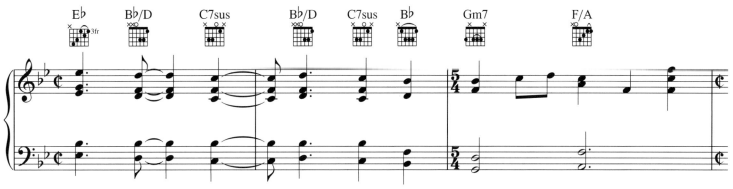

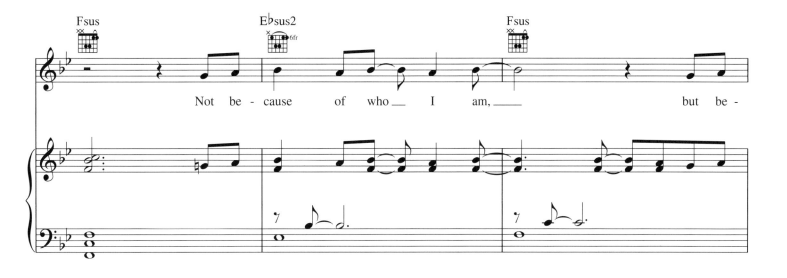

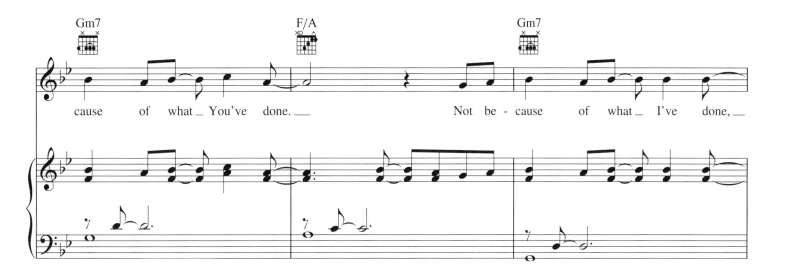

but be-cause of who ___ You are. _____

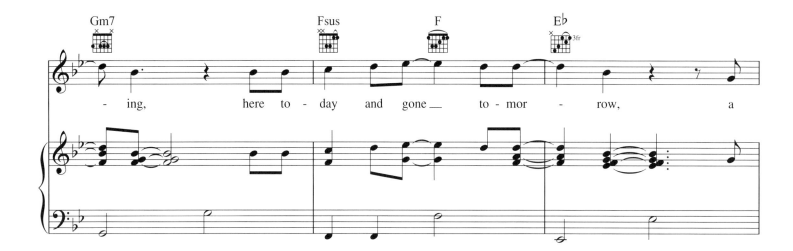

_____ I am a flow-er quick-ly fad-

-ing, here to-day and gone ___ to-mor-row, a

wave tossed ___ in the o-cean, a va-por in ___ the wind. ___

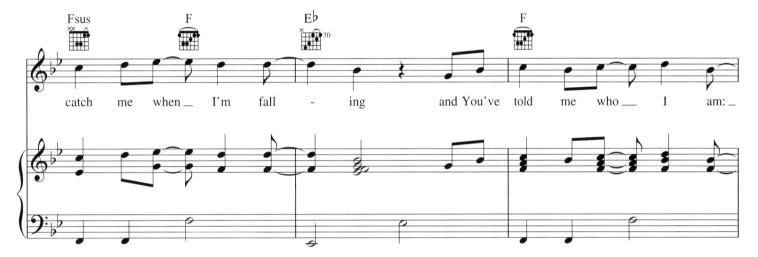

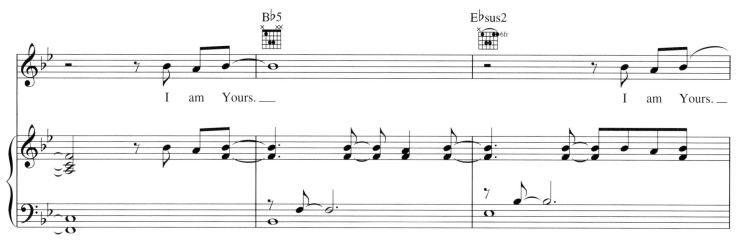

I am Yours. ___   I am Yours. ___

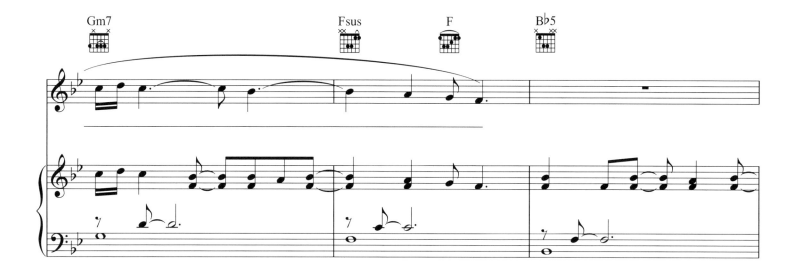

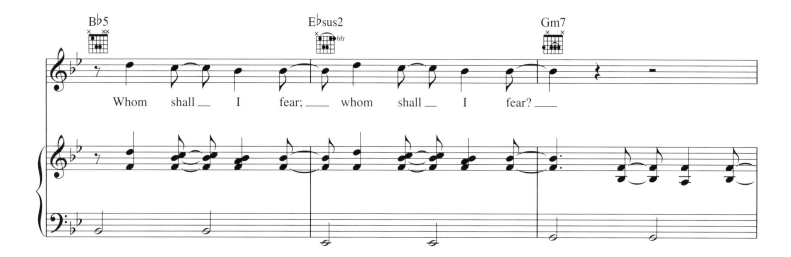

Whom shall __ I fear; ___ whom shall __ I fear? ___

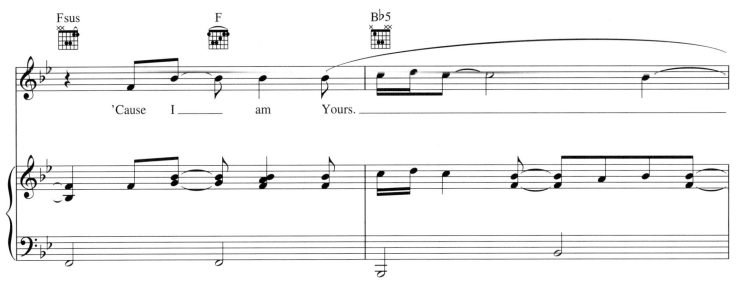

'Cause I _____ am Yours. _____

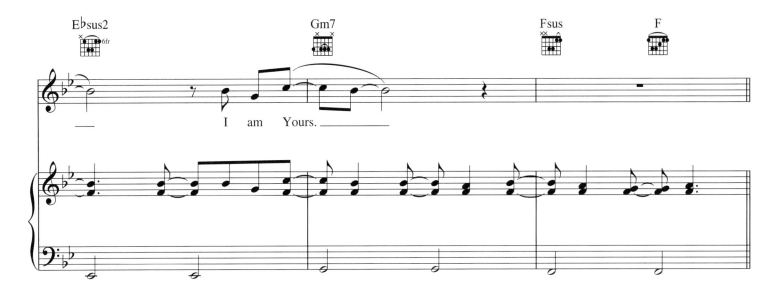

_____ I am Yours. _____

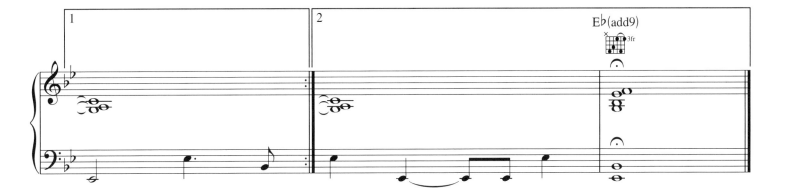

THE ULTIMATE SONGBOOKS

HAL•LEONARD®
PIANO PLAY-ALONG

AUDIO ACCESS INCLUDED

These great songbook/audio packs come with our standard arrangements for piano and voice with guitar chord frames plus audio.

The audio includes a full performance of each song, as well as a second track without the piano part so you can play "lead" with the band! Volumes 86 and beyond also include the Amazing Slow Downer technology so PC and Mac users can adjust the recording to any tempo without changing the pitch! Packs include CDs unless otherwise marked.

HAL•LEONARD®
CORPORATION
7777 W. Bluemound Rd. P.O. Box 13819
Milwaukee, Wisconsin 53213

Visit Hal Leonard Online at
www.halleonard.com

Prices, contents and availability subject to change without notice.
Disney characters and artwork © Disney Enterprises, Inc.

0116